John Wesley
AND THE
METHODISTS

BY CYRIL DAVEY

Marshall Morgan & Scott/Abingdon Press

Fire!

John Wesley and the Methodist Church

John Wesley died on 2nd March, 1791, at the age of eighty-eight. No man in England was better known — nor did any man of his time know at first-hand England, and much of Scotland and Wales, as he did. He had travelled constantly every part of the country, especially its towns and growing industrial areas, riding some 300,000 miles by horse and in his later years by coach, in the fifty years of his astonishing ministry. Wesley's life almost spanned the century; and more than most of its politicians, thinkers and writers he helped to transform the nation. The effects, both religious and social, of the Evangelical Revival, in which Methodism was by far the largest and most vigorous element, lived on through the next two centuries and spread not only across the Atlantic but around the world.

Looking back at the end of his long, full life, John Wesley could only find one phrase to sum it all up: 'What hath God wrought!'

Epworth Rectory

John Wesley was born on 28th June, 1703 — the fifteenth child, but only the second son, of Samuel Wesley, rector of Epworth in Lincolnshire, and his wife Susanna. Not all the children survived, and three more were born after him. Charles Wesley was born in 1707 and until his death in 1788 was John's closest friend, most devoted colleague and sometimes his sharpest critic.

Lincolnshire had always been fen country, and three centuries ago Epworth was a small town set in an area of marshes and swamps, where villages were isolated by flooding for half the year. The population, mostly illiterate, lived in squalor and poverty on a meager diet and accepted as a matter of course the high death rate among children. What was true of Lincolnshire was true of rural England as a whole and, as the eighteenth century progressed, the expanding industrial areas fared even worse. The aristocracy, with their wealth and great houses, were unmoved to pity or reform.

Susanna Wesley was an intellectual woman, strong-minded, and a good housekeeper on an income quite insufficient for her large family, who ruled them all with strict discipline. They were trained 'to cry softly and fear the rod', and undoubtedly to keep themselves unspotted from the world of the crude peasantry who resented the 'gentleman rector' and his sermons against their sins. Their mother taught them in the rectory kitchen — the alphabet had to be learned on their fifth

Portrait of Susanna, mother of John Wesley. A formidable woman, she had a family of nineteen children.

birthday and they started reading the next day — for six hours a day, with a curriculum ranging from the Scriptures to the classics. John was quick, obedient and logical, wanting to know the reason for everything; a trait that would mark his long search for religious reality and characterize his later ministry.

'A brand plucked from the burning!'

When he was five there was a near-tragedy. The rectory caught fire and, though the rest of the family managed to escape, John was unable to get down the burning staircase from the top storey. He dragged a chair to the window, climbed on it, called for help and waited calmly until he was lifted down. For once his mother's

The Epworth Rectory was rebuilt after the fire, and is today open to the public as a Wesley museum.

The five-year-old John Wesley is rescued from the inferno at Epworth Rectory, 9 February 1709.

austerity broke down, as they all prayed thankfully together in the farmyard. Turning to Scripture for the right phrase, she thanked God for this 'brand plucked from the burning' and assured the small boy that God had saved him 'for a purpose'. John's logical mind never doubted it.

In the rebuilt rectory, literature, politics, his father's poetry and Scripture commentaries were the stuff of conversation. This was not a family hedged in by merely rural interests, and John's older brother Samuel, who had gone to Westminster School and then to Oxford, whetted John's desire for a larger world. In 1714, age eleven, he was sent to London to Charterhouse, the public school, and, writing home, told his family that he ran

three times round the school yard each morning, which gave him an appetite for what the big boys had not stolen from his rations. His family, in turn, reported the haunting of the rectory by the poltergeist, 'Old Jeffery', which made John wish he were at home.

A careless student

Then, at seventeen, well-equipped in Latin and Greek, John went up to Oxford. While only members of the Church of England, however nominal, were admitted to the universities at that period, this meant nothing in terms of faith or practice, and though Wesley shared none of the vices of the typical undergraduate he was, as he confessed, 'careless' and extravagant, often needing help from his poverty-stricken father. The real difference from his contemporaries was in his dedication to hard and wide study.

The dreaming spires of Oxford. John Wesley entered Christ Church College in 1720 as a scholar, and later returned to Lincoln College as a fellow.

Ordained a deacon in 1725, John was made a Fellow of Lincoln College the next year. Twice over the next three years he obtained leave of absence to help his aging father at Epworth, taking the curacy of the neighboring village of Wroote. But while there were bucolic pleasures, even in Lincolnshire, there was nothing to stimulate his academic interests or the quest for religious reality which was beginning to stir within him. If there was one thing lacking in the Established Church at this time it was the passion that came from an inward experience of Christ.

Charterhouse, London. John Wesley won a place at Charterhouse School at the age of ten.

An engraving of the Holy Club in session at Oxford. Among those listening to John Wesley are George Whitefield, James Harvey, Robert Kirkham, Benjamin Ingham, William Morgan and John Gambold.

General James Oglethorpe (1696-1785), who sailed to North America to found the new colony of Georgia. John and Charles Wesley went with him as missionaries to the Indians.

Anglican religion was totally formal; 'enthusiasm' (of which Wesley and the Methodists were later constantly accused) was rejected and abhorred. Theology was cold, with a strong tendency to Deism — the acknowledgment only of a remote and uninterested 'sustainer of the universe'. Worship was dreadfully dull. Morning prayer without evening service was the norm, with no hymns, and psalms perhaps droned out by the parish clerk alone. Holy Communion was usually administered once a quarter. Preaching was negligible, in quantity and quality. Many clergy were 'absentees', living in London or on their estates, while under-paid, ill-educated curates cared for the sheep who were so ill-fed. In the new towns, later in the century, the populations were almost totally unchurched.

In 1729, having been ordained priest the previous year, John Wesley was recalled by Oxford University to lecture in Greek, philosophy and logic. But by this time his brother Charles had gone up to Christ Church. John entered a new situation.

The 'Holy Club'

Charles, deeply religious, had gathered together a group of like-minded conscientious men for regular Bible-study in his rooms. Given various names by ribald undergraduates, the most popular was the contemptuous 'Holy Club', though the one that lived on into the future

was 'Methodists', from their orderly life of prayer, worship and service to the poor. Among the members was George Whitefield, an innkeeper's son from Gloucester, who would later set John Wesley's feet on 'the road to revival'. Their 'service' included visiting the poor in the city; caring for the sick; organizing classes for poor children; visiting the prisons; and standing by the criminals when they were hanged. One Holy Club member wrote that 'Mr Wesley was always the chief manager'.

Outside his preoccupation with the Holy Club, John was always busily occupied, and his reading list for six months included sixty major books, some of them in Latin, Greek or Hebrew. His future, however, was still far from clear. When his brother Samuel tried to persuade him to take over from his father as rector of Epworth, he said he preferred Oxford — he might have added that he disliked the fens and the people — but he was less wedded to Oxford than he claimed and more restive in spirit than he admitted. The religion of the Holy Club did not go deep enough. He was in religious turmoil, examining his own soul but finding neither joy nor peace. He was soon to plunge yet deeper into despair.

'Who shall convert me?'

In 1732 General Oglethorpe, a distinguished soldier and prison-reformer, agreed to undertake the organization of a new colony in America, to be named Georgia, and, since he knew the Wesley brothers, they set out with him for the New World in 1735. Charles was to be his secretary and John chaplain to the colonists and, he hoped, missionary to the Indians. But John was really going, he wrote, 'in the hopes of saving my own soul'.

His hopes were not fulfilled and, for both brothers, the American interlude was a disastrous failure. John returned to England in 1737, a little later than his brother, much sadder but no wiser. His rigid high churchmanship, rigorous disciplinary actions, and coldness of temperament to his congregation, proved him precisely the wrong sort of man to deal with the new colonists. His brief exchanges with the Indians were equally inept.

One thing of great importance did happen. The calmness of a group of German Moravians, in a storm that he thought would wreck the ship, impressed Wesley deeply. In Georgia he found them to possess a joy in their religion that he could hardly understand. Back in London he met with Moravians again in their small, intimate meetings and found that their calmness and joy both came from what

they described as 'an assurance of salvation'. Both the words and the demeanor of the Moravians haunted him through the following months. On the voyage home he had written in his *Journal*: 'I went to America to convert the Indians, but, oh, who shall convert me?' Now he was ready for a rearrangement of his whole life and thinking. The search was nearing its end.

Above: An artist's impression of the young John Wesley preaching to the North American Indians.

Below: The Wesley Room, Lincoln College, Oxford, restored to an eighteenth century style by American Methodists. This room was not in fact Wesley's.

Assurance!

On Whit Sunday, 1738, Charles Wesley entered into a new experience and must have shared his glorious certainties with his brother. Three days later John had the experience which was to change his life and very soon began to change England. This is how he describes it in his *Journal* for the 24th May:

'In the evening I went very unwillingly to a society in Aldersgate Street, where one was reading Luther's preface to the Epistle to the Romans. About a quarter before nine, while he was describing the change which God works in the heart through faith in Christ, I felt my heart strangely warmed, I felt I did trust in Christ, Christ alone, for salvation; and an assurance was given me that he had taken away my sins, even mine, and saved me from the law of sin and death.'

Immediately he went round to Charles's lodgings in Little Britain, not far away, to tell him that he, too, had found the liberating gift of faith and grace. Charles was recovering from an attack of pleurisy but together they sat and sang the hymn which Charles had just written to express the experience which his brother now shared:

Where shall my wondering soul begin?
How shall I all to heaven aspire?
A slave redeemed from death and sin,
A brand plucked from eternal fire,
How shall I equal triumphs raise,
Or sing my great Deliverer's praise?

John's mind must have gone back to his childhood as he sang the line that reminded him that he was indeed 'a brand plucked from the burning'. But the *purpose* of his being saved, in Epworth and again this May evening, appears in another verse of the hymn they sang. He is no longer a slave, but a son; and equally he is not saved to provide himself with a sense of peace and joy, but to share it with others:

'The Banquet', from William Hogarth's series of paintings of eighteenth century election scenes, reflects the corruption and decadence of public life at that time.

Outcasts of men, to you I call,
    Harlots, and publicans, and thieves!
He spreads his arms to embrace you all;
    Sinners alone his grace receive;
No need of him the righteous have;
He came the lost to seek and save.

But how was the gospel invitation to *all* to be made known? For the time being there was no clear directive and it was to be almost a year before the way was plain.

The Enthusiasts

In the months that followed, John met with small groups, including Moravians, as they explored the spiritual and devotional life. These groups were known as 'societies', additional to and not competitors with the Church, and were to become particularly characteristic of Methodism. On Sundays, the brothers at first preached widely in London pulpits — but not for long. Their sermons were intolerable to 'respectable' congregations accustomed to dull or inaudible platitudes, for they not only preached about personal salvation but about personal and social sin — the carelessness and licence which were the normal habit of life. Pulpit after pulpit was closed to them because of their 'excesses' and 'enthusiasm'.

Still uncertain of their future, they remained in London, John living on his continuing income as an Oxford 'Fellow'. Some of their Holy Club friends had become parish priests — a course neither of the brothers wished to follow — and one, George Whitefield, was already one of the most notable preachers in England and America, an orator of tremendous power. Indeed the great actor David Garrick once said: 'I would give a hundred guineas if I could say "Oh" like Mr Whitefield!'

Now this itinerant preacher was again in England and what he was doing in Bristol shocked all who heard of it, not least the Wesleys. He was preaching *in the open air* to Kingswood miners and to all who would listen! More, he assured John, he was seeing their lives changed. Then, while the brothers were expressing their abhorrence of their friend's breach of Anglican decencies, Whitefield sent John an urgent message. He himself must return to America . . . would John come and continue the work he had begun so successfully? Charles argued against it; John was critical and resistant, but in the end he rode off to Bristol with two

companions 'to see what was happening'.

There, he was both repelled by the rough men who gathered round Whitefield and much moved by their response to his preaching, but something within himself made it impossible to ride away again from his dilemma.

Above: George Whitefield, a celebrated preacher of the age; his rhetorical gifts were the envy of the actor David Garrick.

Break-through and break-away

On Monday, 2nd April 1739, John Wesley took his most decisive step since his visit to the Aldersgate society:

'I could scarce reconcile myself to this strange way of preaching in the fields of which (Whitefield) set me an example on Sunday; having been all my life (till very lately) so tenacious of every point relating to decency and order, that I should have believed the saving of souls almost a sin, if it had not been done in a church . . . at four in the afternoon I made myself more vile and proclaimed in the highways the glad tidings of salvation . . . speaking from a little eminence in the ground adjoining the city, to about three thousand people.'

His text, deeply appropriate, was: 'The Spirit of the Lord is upon me, because he has anointed me to preach the gospel to the poor'.

Below: An artist's impression of John Wesley preaching.

Opposite: This statue of John Wesley on horseback stands outside the preacher's stable at the New Room, Bristol. Wesley read avidly on his long rides across the country.

The interior of the New Room, Bristol, the first Methodist meeting-house.

The entrance and preacher's stable, the New Room, Bristol.

In calling for Wesley to continue his Bristol ministry, Whitefield had hoped that he would 'confirm those that were already awakened'. So, indeed, he did. But he did far more. In the ten days that followed that momentous Monday break-through, he met with half a dozen 'societies'; gathered small groups of men and women who were prepared to meet together for mutual confession and 'healing of their souls' (the beginnings of the Methodist class-meeting); preached twice in prison; and spoke six times in the open-air, including a visit to Bath, to some fifteen thousand people. The crowds who came to listen to this calm, neat, un-dramatic little Oxford don in Anglican preaching-robes were as large as those who followed Whitefield, and soon were even greater, and the results were at least as dramatic. In the early days those who were 'convicted of sin' passed through shat-tering psychological disturbances before they came into calmness and peace, though these phenomena were typical only of the earlier days of the revival. Wesley followed up conversion by demanding that it *must* be confirmed by changed habits of life.

That April afternoon when Wesley broke through his ingrained Anglican trad-itionalism and spoke for the first time 'in the fields' marked the very beginning of the Methodist revival.

He stayed in Bristol for two months, always preaching in the open-air since no church would open its doors to him, and in May bought a small piece of ground in the Horsefair where a room was to be built for the growing 'societies' gathered from his new converts. Rebuilt some four years later as the first Methodist preaching-house in the world, John Wesley's 'New Room' still stands in Bristol's busy shopping-centre at Broadmead.

The Foundery opens

In June he rode back to London for the first time, and immediately began the same sort of ministry he had had in Bristol — open-air preaching; setting up societies meeting weekly under a lay-leader; and the purchase of a disused foundery for use as a preaching-house and a home for elderly women including his widowed mother. The Foundery was to be the centre of London Methodism until he opened his new chapel in City Road in 1778.

Charles was critical of his brother's open-air ministry but still very supportive of what was clearly a work of God, and throughout the rest of their lives the two men were to be the joint leaders of the Methodist revival. Until Charles's marriage in 1748 they itinerated, separately or occasionally together, preaching throughout the country. It is because John, despite his own uneasy marriage, continued to travel, preach and organize until his death that he is commonly regarded as the 'creator' of Methodism. The phrase is undoubtedly just and deserved.

In the two years following John's first Bristol minstry they divided the responsi-bility for London and Bristol between them. More emotional than John, Charles was a preacher of considerable power and, faced with the challenge of unchurched multitudes, he at last 'broke down the bridge and became desperate'. 'I found ten thousand helpless sinners waiting for the word in Moorfields (London) . . . the Lord was with me . . . my load was gone and all my doubts and scruples'. In London, Bristol and the intervening countryside they never stopped preaching.

'Joy in the Holy Ghost'

Whether they knew it or not they were not alone in the new surge of revival. Laymen such as John Nelson in the West Riding,

John Bennett in Lancashire and Cheshire, John Haime in the Army and others were already doing the same sort of work, and some were to be drawn in by Wesley as his colleagues. But by 1742 it was plain to them both that the whole of England was in need of their gospel of grace. In May that year John rode off north and reached Newcastle eight days later, having preached throughout the journey. Newcastle was soon to become the third hub of the Methodist system, with strong societies and an orphan-house, an early sign of Wesley's practical concern with the poor.

On his way back he stopped at Epworth. There, 'a little before the service began I went to Mr Romley, the curate, and offered to assist him by preaching or reading prayers; but he did not care to accept of my assistance.' Indeed, the curate preached vehemently against 'enthusiasm'. But that was not the end. 'At six I came, and found such a congregation as I believe Epworth never saw before. I stood . . . upon my father's tombstone, and cried, "The kingdom of heaven is not meat and drink; but righteousness, and peace, and joy in the Holy Ghost".'

That single incident is typical of John Wesley's reception by the church throughout his travels, and equally so of his own response and of the scriptural basis of his preaching.

Riding with the gospel

His travels with the gospel had begun. The year 1742 included several rides to Bristol, Wales, the Midlands, and back to Newcastle-upon-Tyne in the wintry weather of November — but throughout his life, bad weather never discouraged him. The following year he was back again in the Midlands, Yorkshire and the North, and in August set off on the first of his 32 visits to Cornwall. He kept a careful record of his travels, in shorthand, in his private diaries which were later expanded and published in his famous *Journal*. More and more crowded itineraries, including Scotland and Ireland, fill the pages.

Often he preached four or five times a day, beginning at five in the morning. He could be seen speaking on village greens, in town squares, outside private houses or on a stool in front of an inn. And not only seen, but heard, too, for his voice had an extreme clarity and carrying-power; indeed, by careful measurement he once found he could be heard at a distance of 140 yards. With all this preaching he made time for

Wesley the preacher.

private conversation, too, constantly, in his favorite phrase 'offering Christ'; for closely examining the work of his preachers and the way members of the societies kept the rules; and occasionally for social engagements and visiting places of interest. And, wherever he rode, he read unceasingly, leaving his horse with a loose rein to find its own way along the rough tracks. Within a decade hardly any man was more familiar in every part of Britain.

A movement grows

Methodism, the popular name for the new movement, spread more and more widely and its membership grew year by year. Those who joined the societies were sinners who had found salvation, and their own witness in word and life added yet more to the numbers, while his 'helpers' — laymen-preachers — whom he stationed through Britain and Ireland to minister to the increasing number of converts gathered in yet more from the unchurched, underprivileged common people.

The swift growth of such an unconventional movement attracted both resistance and persecution, and while rowdy elements in the crowds may have been the agents of disturbance, it was almost always the clergy and the 'gentry' who were its instigators. The early years of Methodism were a period of political insecurity and general fear. The new Hanoverian Protestant kings of England, George I and II, sat on uneasy thrones for it was generally

Wesley caught in a riot at Wednesbury, Staffordshire.

believed that subversive plotters were determined to restore the exiled Roman Catholic Stuarts to the monarchy. The unsuccessful 1715 invasion, followed by the abortive 1745 rebellion, made it all too easy to persuade simple people that the Wesleys were 'Jacobites in disguise' seeking to overthrow king and government.

Persecution!

But, in the main, the opposition was not politically motivated. The gentry resented their stirring up the common people, fearing an assertion of rights denied them everywhere, while the clergy opposed them for a variety of reasons — doubts about their theology, or about their unconventional methods; resentment at their preaching in other men's parishes; and, not infrequently, out of sheer malice.

Despite the general antipathy of the church, however, the Methodists had the sympathy and support of a number of able, dedicated clergy in several parts of the country. They included the saintly John Fletcher of Madeley, whom Wesley saw for a time as his natural successor; Vincent Perronet of Shoreham; and the eccentric William Grimshaw of Haworth. All these, and others, saw and sustained revival in their own parishes.

Persecution was sporadic rather than universal, but where it broke out it could be

dangerous. Wesley's *Journal* entries are vivid and frightening. 'Gentlemen' set the press-gang on him. Cattle were driven into his open-air meetings, or drummers marched through them. Less violently, a harlequin climbed a pole in Moorfields to distract attention. Mobs broke into private houses to attack the preachers. The Wesleys remained outwardly calm, disarmed the ringleaders by their courage, and often, having silenced them, saw them 'turn like lambs' to become as vehement in their defense as they had been in attack.

Mob violence, frequent in the early years of the rivival, practically died out by the 1750s, though local Methodists still had to suffer. 'The zealous landlord', noted Wesley, 'turned all the Methodists out of their homes'.

'Only let me alone with the poor . . .'

There were some areas of Britain where even the ardent Wesley never preached. Much of Devon, for instance, was hardly touched by the revival. His preachers were urged to go not to those who needed them, 'but to those who need you most', and though he well knew people everywhere were in need of the gospel, the under-populated rural areas did not offer the same opportunities that he found in and around the towns, and it was there that he made his greatest impact. Those who responded to the Methodist preaching were mostly what were regarded as 'the lower orders', not generally acceptable in the parish churches — the province of 'the better classes' — even after their characters and habits were transformed by evangelical conversion.

Wesley always yearned with pity for the poor. In an open letter to the clergy he wrote: 'The rich, the honourable, the great, we willingly leave to you. Only let us alone with the poor, the vulgar, the base, the outcasts of men.' Their condition should have torn anyone's heart. 'Throughout Cornwall, in the north, even in the midlands . . . I have seen wretched creatures, totally unemployed, standing in the streets, with pale looks, hollow eyes,

A detail from 'The Banquet' by Hogarth.

and meager limbs, or creeping up and down like walking shadows.' That was in a sermon as late as 1775. Nor did he condescend from above. When in London he lived, as did his London preachers, at his own Poor House, 'with nine widows, two poor children, one blind woman and two upper servants — an earnest of our eating bread together in the kingdom of heaven'.

But 'the poor', the ordinary working people and artisans, proved themselves men and women of real ability as well as spiritual quality. In Bristol, for instance, his 'local' preachers included '2 hoopers, 2 weavers, 2 braziers, a serge maker, a carpenter . . . etc.'

'The world is my parish'

Wesley had no intention that his movement should compete with the Established Church and, indeed, hoped that Methodism would be accepted in it and help to revive it. But inevitably Methodism grew up *alongside*, if not deliberately outside, the parish churches. It developed its own organization (as a later section will clearly show) and, equally important, Wesley never diminished any of his own authority within it. In particular he refused to consider limiting his itinerant ministry. He had stated his commission to Bishop Butler of Bristol in the early days of the revival: 'The world is my parish'.

It would be tediously repetitive to follow the detailed progress of the Methodist revival. There were, of course, constant problems, many of them arising from the tensions between his preachers and their authoritarian leader, or between Wesley and the trustees of the chapels which were all legally held in his own name. There were financial difficulties in local societies. There was a deepening difference of opinion with his loved brother, Charles, about the 'drift away from the Anglican church'. Nevertheless, Methodism achieved a steady growth without deceptive moments of glory. In general, the Methodist story is of constant expansion throughout the century; of the emergence within it and through its own religious emphases, from the illiterate peasantry and industrial workers, of a middle class with sober habits, sound family life and sturdy independence. In particular it is dominated by the personality and creative leadership of one man, John Wesley.

'Let me never live to be useless'

Charles Wesley died in London in 1788. Deeply revered and loved in Methodism, he was not, and never set out to be, the leader that his brother had become. Indeed, he was sternly critical of John's authoritarian, individualistic actions. Charles lived in London in the midst of a circle of friends, who responded to a warm disposition very different from his brother's. He had achieved his own notable reputation as poet and musician, and fathered two brilliant musicians in his sons Samuel and Charles, while his grandson, Samuel Sebastian, was to be yet more distinguished in the world of music.

So poor were communications, that news of his death did not reach John until after his funeral. John was deeply affected by the loss, but he himself did not have many more years to live. A few years before his death he wrote in his *Journal* on his birthday: 'Lord, let me never live to be useless.' His prayer was answered. He was preaching, meeting people, writing letters, almost to the end. He had once written that he did not expect Methodism to last for more than twenty or thirty years, yet it was stronger than ever, an ineradicable part of the religious life of England.

In 1791, when he died, there were 72,000 members in the British Methodism and probably three times as many adherents. In addition there were about the same number in the United States and the West Indies.

Why?

It is, in human terms, an extraordinary achievement arising from the evangelical experience and leadership of one man. The question that arises is inevitable. Why this phenomenal 'success'?

There are many answers, but, apart from the stupendous effect of Charles Wesley's hymns, most of them derive from John Wesley — his preaching, his genius for organization, his voluminous writing and publishing, the breadth of his social concern, but most of all from the quality of the man himself. In the next few pages, we shall look at each of these elements in turn.

In appearance Wesley was short in stature, slim, controlled in gesture and movement. His hair was dark, neatly parted in the center, worn long to avoid the expense of elaborate hairdressing and, contrary to custom, he never wore a wig. Indeed he made no concessions to fashion in his dress and once wrote that he was always to be found in a short coat or a cassock and gown or, at home, in a 'dressing-gown'. For so small a man he had a voice of remarkable authority, which, indeed, matched his normal demeanor.

'Nothing without reason'

What he lacked in height he certainly made up in intellectual dominance and especially in a clear, cool and logical mind. As a child he 'would do nothing without reason', as his father said with irritation, and if in later years he was persuaded there was sound reason for a decision or action, neither opposition not sentiment would deter him. He was methodical in all he undertook, and in every part of his life. Two examples of his self-discipline, for example, are to be found in his use of time and money. He always rose at four in the morning and immediately devoted himself to the study of the Scriptures and to prayer — but was nevertheless ready to preach at five o'clock.

He was the perfect example of his own rule for his preachers: 'Be never unemployed; be never triflingly employed.'

His personal practice about money he explained in print and, writing as if of someone else, this is what he said: '. . . had thirty pounds a year income' (when he was at Oxford). 'He lived on twenty-eight and gave away forty shillings. The next year receiving sixty pounds he still lived on twenty-eight and gave away two and thirty. The third year he received ninety pounds and gave away sixty-two. The fourth year he received a hundred and twenty pounds. Still, he lived as before on twenty-eight and gave to the poor ninety-two.'

It was a discipline he followed to the end of his life. He earned a great deal from his books — his friend Henry Moore estimated that he must have given away more than £32,000 in his lifetime — and died with almost nothing.

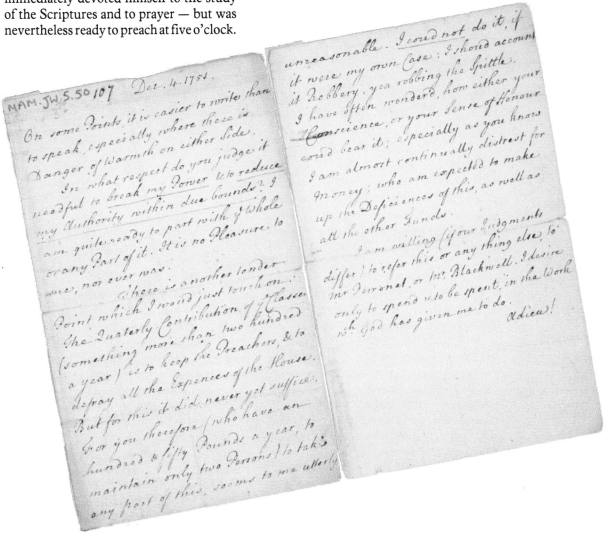

A letter from John Wesley to his brother Charles, dated 4 December 1751.

There was nothing narrow about his interests, except in 'frivolous pleasures'. His reading was by no means all theological or religious. He was fascinated by the new as well as the old — as, for instance, in his setting up at one of his London dispensaries an 'electrical machine' which he used for simple 'shock treatment' for his patients.

He was cool but not cold, objective rather than emotional, perhaps more revered than loved. Certainly with his upbringing, temperament and rational intellect he could well have become a rigorous, academic High Churchman, with preferment at Oxford or as a bishop. It was his Aldersgate experience which changed everything — transformed the man, enriched his emotions and gave him a gospel of hope and love. For ever afterwards nothing robbed him of the certainty that he had a personal experience of God's grace, an unshakable 'inward assurance' by the Spirit of his redemption in Christ. This left him with an unremitting dedication to God's purpose, wherever it might take him and whatever the difficulties or dangers involved. For him that purpose was summed up as 'the spreading of Scriptural Holiness throughout the land'.

The preacher

The interior of City Road Chapel, London — the cathedral of Methodism.

The preaching don

The second element contributing to Methodist growth — perhaps the primary one for contemporary observers — was Wesley's preaching. It was what he said, rather than the strange sight of an Oxford don preaching in the streets, that held people and changed their lives.

His speech was vigorous, plain and direct. He did not conduct open-air *worship,* but plunged immediately into what he had to say, always speaking from Scripture. There were no emotional trappings, illustrations or stories. His method was to expound the Bible with logical argument and to press home his message on two fronts — the grace of God for sinners, and the change in life that this must produce in those who believed. He faced his hearers with their sins, and 'offered Christ' with forgiveness and assurance for those who repented. Always he expected the ordinary, uneducated people who were mostly his hearers to understand what he said without ever 'speaking down' to them. His universal gospel of salvation was in direct contrast to the narrow exclusiveness of contemporary Calvinism or the remoteness of Deism. He was the very opposite of the usual mumbling parish cleric.

Notably, what he said went home to his hearers' hearts. He *expected* people to be changed, by God's grace — and they were. He expected them to grow in pace, and offered Christian perfection as an attainable goal, though he himself never claimed to have reached it. He demanded that those who were converted should 'build each other up' in the weekly 'class-meeting' and in regular worship, and that their lives should witness to their faith. He never offered heaven as an 'alternative' to earthly joy but as a fulfilment of discipleship; and if Methodist standards of life and behaviour were puritanical, in contrast to today, they were readily accepted and passed on, not least within the family unit.

THE WORLD IS MY PARISH.

Charles Wesley, John's hymn-writer brother.

Charles Wesley

'Born in song'

If this seems a rigid sort of existence for new Christians, the early Methodists exulted in it — and they had a fresh and exciting way of expressing their experience. Charles Wesley's hymns were his own unique contribution to the revival.

Charles Wesley wrote some 6,000 hymns and though, in this immense number, there was much 'trite versification of evangelical commonplace', the same critic continues to say 'they remain the finest body of devotional verse in the English language'. What the average reader may not recognize is how fully his hymns reflect the language of the Bible, with half-a-dozen Scripture passages providing the images of as many lines, at times.

But if they were poetry they were certainly written to be sung. He used, or invented, every meter it was possible to set to singable tunes; and many of the tunes he used were vigorous, well-known and easily sung, including operative arias and popular songs. Handel himself composed half a dozen tunes for Charles's hymns, including 'Rejoice, the Lord is King!' His hymns live on today and no modern hymn-book would be complete without 'Hark, the Herald Angels Sing', 'Christ the Lord is Risen Today', or 'Jesu, Lover of my Soul'. 'Gentle, Jesus, Meek and Mild' was the most popular hymn for children for a century or more, while 'Soldiers of Christ, Arise', written with the sound of an anti-Methodist riot in his ears, remains a

Charles Wesley's house at Charles Street, Bristol, his home for twenty years.

Charles Wesley's organ, which is preserved today at The Foundery Chapel, London.

rousing call to Christian action.

It has been truly said that 'Methodism was born in song' and undoubtedly these hymns differentiated it from every other part of the eighteenth-century church. Its members sang out their faith, fears, resolutions and triumphs week by week, often with a vigour unparalleled anywhere else. The joy of the music denied the criticisms of those who described Methodists as somber misery makers. Not for nothing was this the first hymn in the Methodist hymnbook for more than two centuries:

O for a thousand tongues to sing
  My great Redeemer's praise,
The glories of my God and King,
  The triumphs of his grace!

The subjects might be deeply serious, but the unusual meters and rhythms Charles used lifted the hearts and moved the feet of those who sang a hymn like this:

O God of all grace,
  Thy goodness we praise:
Thy Son Thou has given to die in our
  place.
  He came from above
  Our curse to remove;

A modern statue of Charles Wesley, standing outside the New Room, Bristol.

Charles Wesley's original manuscript for his famous hymn 'Love Divine, All Loves Excelling'.

He hath loved, he hath loved us, because he would love.

In some cases he managed to encapsulate almost all the essential doctrines of the Methodist revival in a single verse, such as in this hymn which begins: 'Spirit of faith, come down,':

Inspire the living faith,
Which whosoe'er receives,
The witness in himself he hath,
And consciously believes;
The faith that conquers all,
And doth the mountains move,
And saves whoe'er on Jesus call,
And perfects them in love.

In that verse he points to the central Methodist doctrines of 'the witness of the Spirit', 'justification by faith', and 'Christian perfection' with hints of others, too.

Notably he reiterated, in hymn after hymn, his brother's lifelong proclamation of the universality of the gospel. One of his characteristic words, which sounds bell-like in line after line, is 'all'. He writes:

His sovereign grace extends to all,
And:
For all my Lord was crucified,
For all, for all, my Saviour died.
And yet more resonantly:
Sent by my Lord, on you I call;
The invitation is to all;
Come all the world, come sinner thou;
All things in Christ are ready now.

It is easy to see why John Wesley published four hymn-books during his lifetime, and why they all included so many of Charles's hymns. But, practical as ever, John tried to ensure that congregations sang them properly! In his 1770 hymn-book he gave very clear instructions at some length, in his customary precise style, on 'How to sing'. Even without the full text the headings show his mind. 'Sing all . . . Sing lustily . . . Sing modestly . . . Sing in time . . . Above all, sing spiritually — attend strictly to what you sing and see that your heart is not carried away with the sound.'

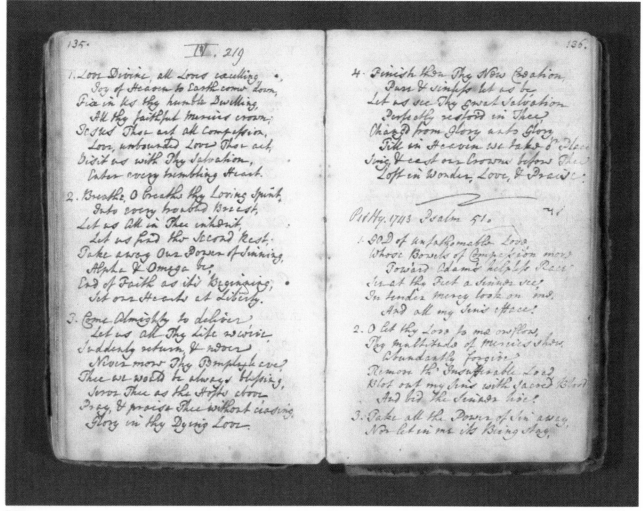

The Methodists

On the human side, John Wesley's practicality determined the stability and progress of Methodism. He had a genius for organization. With no carefully designed campaign of evangelism and consolidation, he reacted to needs and situations as they emerged, and many of his experiments were so logical and practical that they became basic to the continuing structure of Methodism. Had it not been so, the effects of his preaching would probably have been local and transitory, while Charles's hymns would have produced an exuberance that was equally short-lived. Authoritarian by nature, John expected to be obeyed. His critics, in the latter part of his ministry, who dubbed him 'Pope John', were both restive and right. But although he rode his horse with a loose rein he knew instinctively that only a firm hand could keep Methodism on what he believed to be the right road.

'The Society of People called Methodists'—Wesley's own name—knew it had very clearly defined standards, and he wrote the 'rules for members' himself. The 'one condition required' was 'a desire to flee from the wrath to come, to be saved from their sins. But . . . it will be shown by its fruits. It is therefore expected . . .'

What was expected fell under three heads: doing no harm, doing good, attending upon the ordinances of God. The last included public worship, the sacraments, private devotions and fasting. 'Doing good to all men' naturally involved Christian service, but with practical realism, the support of fellow Methodists in trade and business. 'Doing no harm' ranged from avoiding drunkenness, going to law and working on Sunday, to buying or selling smuggled goods, 'using many words in buying and selling' and what we would call 'hire-purchase'.

A class system

'Religious societies', small groups for mutual spiritual enrichment, dated from the previous century, and Wesley only continued the useful tradition in setting up local 'Methodist societies'. But he quickly introduced two innovations. He gathered his societies into smaller 'classes' of twelve members — they were called 'society classes' in Methodism for two hundred years — and himself appointed a leader for each class, though later his preachers found the 'class leaders' for the societies under their charge. The classes met each week and discussion was limited to *present* experiences of God's grace in their lives.

The second innovation was a response to the need to find money to replace the first small room in Bristol by 'the New Room'. Every member was asked to pay a penny a week, as did the class-leader, who also paid the pence of those who could not afford it. Self-support was thus early introduced into Methodism, and 'class-money' continued well into the present century.

Apart from field-preaching, the most dramatic challenge to Anglican orderliness came very soon after the work had first begun in Bristol. Delayed in his return to London one night, he found that a young man had broken all the rules by not only reading prayers in the London society but had also expounded the Scriptures. Horrified at first, he was astounded by his mother's declaration that 'Thomas Maxfield has as much right to preach as you have!' Not only so, but he had done it well.

Lay preachers

The result was a far-reaching decision. John and Charles could not really exercise pastoral oversight of all the societies that

City Road Chapel, London, first opened 1 November 1778.

The Prayer Room at John Wesley's House, London. He used to pray here night and morning: 'I sit down alone; my God is here.'

The well-known portrait of John Wesley by Nathaniel Hone.

already existed. There were not enough sympathetic clergy to sustain the revival as it spread across England. He would therefore use lay helpers both to preach and give pastoral care to the new societies. Maxfield was the first of a large band of lay preachers, drawn from a wide range of backgrounds and occupations — over a quarter were ex-soldiers — whom he 'stationed' all over Britain. They were, of course, the predecessors of all the 'Methodist ministers' who followed them, though Wesley himself would never have used the term to describe them. They were his 'helpers'.

Wesley drew up 'Twelve Rules for a Helper' with great care. implicit in them was the fact that they were responsible to Wesley himself and to no one else. Yet, at the same time, they had a great deal of freedom. The rules show that they were expected to preach and look after the flock, but also that they should spend five hours a day in reading — and to those who could

not afford to buy books he gave five pounds with which to do so. He included specific instructions on 'how to preach', and believed that 'softness' supervened when they failed to preach at five in the morning.

The first Conference

Wesley moved his preachers frequently, never allowing them to stay in one place more than three years at the most — another practice that continued in Methodism until the 1940s. Because they 'rode circuit' around the societies in their large districts the groups of chapels to which they were appointed became known as 'circuits', another continuing Methodist term.

In 1744 John and Charles met in London with four Anglican clergymen, all supporters of their work, to 'confer' about the work of the revival. From this small, select beginning grew the annual 'Conference' of preachers, with Wesley presiding over its deliberations; and the 'Conference' remains the ruling body in Methodism, though it is now, of course, a mixed, elected body of lay people, both men and women, and ministers. Of one of Wesley's Conferences an observer wrote: 'There was much concord . . . but Mr Wesley seemed to do all the business himself.'

Despite his innovations, Wesley tried not to compete with the Church he loved and to which he belonged. His preachers might not celebrate Holy Communion, since they were not ordained. It was hoped that Methodists would receive it in their parish church, and it was celebrated by Wesley himself on his itinerations, or by other clergy such as his close colleague, Dr Coke. Methodist services must not be held in 'church hours'; only in the early morning, afternoon or evenings on Sundays. Morning Prayer was the basic early service of Methodism, and Wesley published his own edited version of the Book of Common Prayer, including a 'new' service, the 'Covenant Service', in which his people 'renewed their covenant with God'.

It is nevertheless obvious that, though he refused to admit it, Wesley had created the structure of a new and vigorous denomination. Almost perversely he continued to hope that Methodism would eventually be accepted into the Anglican church. His own defense against the

charge that all he had done led to separation was succinct and heartfelt. In the 1788 Conference, three years before his death, he said: 'We did none of these things till we were convinced we could no longer omit them but at the peril of our souls.'

Charity and education

Wesley believed that 'saving men from hell and fitting them for heaven' was his *primary* task, but equally he never ceased to be concerned about their minds and bodies. He opened an orphanage in Newcastle in the very early days, and began schools in London and other places, but his most conspicuous educational venture was the founding of Kingswood School in Bristol, which became an establishment for the sons of his preachers and, later still, one of Britain's distinguished public schools.

In his book *Primitive Physick* he explained: 'For six or seven and twenty years I made anatomy and physic the diversion of leisure hours', and as a result he established dispensaries for the sick poor. In London he employed an apothecary and an experienced surgeon but fortunately (very differently from his schools where he made all the decisions) he decided 'to leave all difficult and complicated cases to such physicians as the patients might choose'.

A more surprising example of his constructive charity was his 'lending fund' which, with loans ranging from £30 to £120, he administered for some twenty years to relieve workmen, who would otherwise have had to pawn their tools, and for worthy tradesmen in need of help. His 'Stranger's Friend' charity in Bristol and London was specifically for the assistance of those who were *not* Methodists, and still continues today.

Though he was no reformer in the general sense, Wesley campaigned for the reform of prisons, and wrote publicly about the appalling conditions of French prisoners-of-war. Slavery he came to hate and there is a tradition that the reason Cornish Methodists have seldom taken sugar in their tea is because he enjoined them against it since it was gained by slave-labour. The day he wrote his last entry in his private diary he also wrote his last letter — to William Wilberforce, encouraging him in his early campaign against 'that execrable villainy', slavery.

John Wesley preaches from his father's tombstone in Epworth churchyard; a painting by George Washington Brownlow.

Separation

In 1778 he opened his new chapel in London, on City Road, quickly known as 'Wesley's Chapel', and now regarded as the 'cathedral of world Methodism'. Nearby his the tall brick house where he lived the last twelve years of his life and it was there, in 1791, that he died. Almost his last words were: 'The best of all is, God is with us.' Those words appeared almost immediately on cups, mugs, plates and dishes throughout the country, for the souvenir-makers celebrated his death with an output of ceramics that matched that for a military victory or a royal occasion. It was recognized throughout the nation that a very great man had passed away, and had left a notable heritage. Half a century after his first field-preaching in Bristol, Methodism was a well-founded institution, a recognized element in British life.

John Wesley died, he claimed, 'a loyal member of the Church of England'. Yet within thirty years of his death, three dramatic events had happened. The first would have rejoiced his heart; the other two would have saddened him beyond measure. Methodism had established itself in four continents outside of Europe. But at home it had suffered a series of tragic divisions, the first only seven years after he died. Finally, Methodism's separation from the Church of England was complete and, apparently, irrevocable.

The break with the Church of England

Whenever any of his followers raised the question of separation from the Church of England, Wesley relentlessly quashed it. But this, more than anything else, was his 'blind spot' and it was his own 'logic of necessity' which, in effect, ensured the very disruption he rejected.

Under English law, 'Dissenting' preachers and chapels had to be registered to avoid prosecution and, after many years of stubborn resistance, Wesley had to admit that Methodists came into the same legal category as Baptists and Congregationalists. In 1787 he advised that all Methodist preachers and preaching-places should be licensed by

law, and that they should be known as 'Methodist chapels' and 'preachers of the gospel'. This decision, however, had been preceded by two much more radical actions, both of which occurred in 1784.

The first arose from Wesley's very just conviction that no man would be able to 'lead' Methodism as he himself had done. In that year he executed a 'Deed of Declaration' nominating a 'Legal Conference' of one hundred preachers, whose gaps were to be filled annually by its own nominees. *This* was to be his

Wesley's wide-ranging interests included science and medicine; he even owned an electrification machine.

Right: An artist's impression of John Wesley's deathbed. The indefatigable preacher died 2 March 1791.

successor, though without any power until his death. The 'Legal Hundred' was to be the seat of authority in Wesleyan Methodism until it was abolished at Methodist Union in 1932, though it seldom — and never in later years — upset the decisions of the Conference of preachers — and in time laypeople. Constitutionally it ensured the continuance of Methodism.

It was, however, Wesley's other action which was decisive in separating Methodism from its parent-church, for here not merely law but theology was paramount.

When the American War of Independence ended in 1784, almost all the Anglican clergy had fled or been withdrawn from the rebel states. It was almost impossible for anyone to receive Holy Communion from an ordained priest and the American Methodists pressed Wesley to persuade the English bishops to restore some of the clergy. Wesley's pleas were ignored; there was to be no spiritual comfort for the 'rebels'.

Wesley's mind went back to 1746. That year, riding horseback from Bristol to London and reading as he rode, he spent the time on a book by Peter King, later to be Lord Chancellor, which demonstrated to Wesley's complete satisfaction, on the evidence of the New Testament and the Early Church, that a presbyter (or priest) had as much right to ordain as had a bishop. He had believed this for forty years. Now, to remedy the desperate situation in America, he acted on his conviction.

John Wesley's House, next door to City Road Chapel, is today open to the public.

World parish

On 1 September 1784, at 6 Deighton Street, Bristol, he ordained as deacons two Methodist preachers who had been appointed to America, Richard Whatcoat and Thomas Vasey. The next day he ordained them as presbyters to serve the Methodist Church in America and to administer the sacraments. He also 'set apart' Thomas Coke, the Anglican clergyman who had been his very close associate for some time, as 'superintendent' of the work in America. Coke's primary commission was to ordain Francis Asbury, the foremost of the Methodist preachers in America and their acknowledged leader, and with Whatcoat and Vasey he did so at the 'Christmas Conference' in Baltimore a few months later. Asbury himself ws almost immediately styled 'Bishop Asbury' by the new church, as was Coke when he was visiting or travelling in America, though never so in Britain.

Wesley followed these ordinations with others. By 1779 he ordained preachers (though he restricted their right to administer the sacraments to limited areas) for the West Indies and Scotland, and for some remote and rural parts of England. Until his death he continued to ordain a very limited number of preachers for places where the sacraments were almost inaccessible to Methodist people.

Most of Wesley's previous innovations had challenged ecclesiastical conventions and no more than that. Now, however, out of conviction he had rejected the theology on which Anglican (and indeed Catholic) ministerial order was established. In his heart Wesley must have realized that he was creating an order of ministry which could not be accepted by the Anglican church as he knew it. Separation, though delayed, was now inevitable.

After his death the influential preachers who wanted and worked for union with the Church of England carried less and less weight with Conference, which had no wish to 'rejoin' a body of which they had never been part. Ordinations became more frequent. The Church of England made no move to welcome any 'lost sheep' who might return to the fold. Without any formal declaration on either side, Methodism was established as a new church.

A gospel for the whole world

Next to the Wesley brothers themselves, the most significant figure of the period from 1780 to 1814 was Dr Thomas Coke. Born in 1747 in Brecon, South Wales, he was a vigorous, enthusiastic, volatile man; he was also splendidly generous with his substantial financial means. Driven out of his Somerset curacy for 'enthusiasm', he joined Wesley in 1777 and was used in a variety of ways as stand-in for the leader himself. He was a touring evangelist, a trouble-shooter where there were differences between the preachers and the local trustees, a legal expert of great value because of his Oxford D.C.L., and Wesley's regular representative at the Irish Conference.

In 1784, without Wesley's authority, he published *A Plan for the Establishment of Missions amongst the Heathen,* a few years before William Carey made his better-known appeal to found a Baptist missionary society. Wesley did not share Coke's 'intemperate enthusiasm'. His immediate concern was for America, and it was there, that same year, that he sent Coke to ordain Francis Asbury.

Two years later Wesley again sent Coke to America, with three more preachers. The voyage was disastrous and, blown far off course, they made landfall three months after leaving England, on the night of Christmas Eve, at Antigua in the West Indies. At St John's, as he came ashore, Coke met William Baxter, a Methodist shipwright who had continued the work

The house of Nathaniel Gilbert, the Methodist planter, on Antigua.

begun by the Methodist planter, Nathaniel Gilbert, amongst the slaves. At four o'clock that Christmas morning Dr Thomas Coke preached to a thousand Negro slaves gathered for worship! In the weeks that followed he toured the nearby islands, left as missionaries to the slaves the three preachers he should have taken to America and, after his resumed American visit, returned to England to report his actions to a Conference which was deeply moved. Almost at once he was given responsibility as 'Superintendent of Foreign Missions'.

But, while the work spread rapidly through the Caribbean despite hostility from slave-owners and sometimes persecution of the preachers, Coke had yet greater dreams. He could never forget Wesley's first instruction to him. When they had first met and Coke had asked what he should do if he were driven from his parish, the old evangelist had replied: 'Go and preach the gospel to the whole world!'

He wanted to do no less than that. By 1800 he was planning a mission to the East, but it was not until 31 December, 1813, that he sailed from Portsmouth with seven missionaries — for the Cape of Good Hope, Java, India and Ceylon. He himself remained in Ceylon. He never reached his goal.

Coke gave his whole fortune to the missionary cause, very largely sustaining the work in the West Indies by his own gifts. In the end he gave his life to the work he had lived for. He died in May 1814.

His death stirred Methodism perhaps even more deeply than his life had done. Already strongly rooted in the West Indies, Methodist missions were, within a decade, to be found in West and South Africa as well as India and Ceylon, and quickly spread to Australia, New Zealand and the Pacific Islands. The work to which he had called Methodism was to become one of the largest and strongest missionary societies in Europe.

Dr Thomas Coke, one of Wesley's faithful workers, was ordained 'Superintendent of the Societies in America' in 1784.

Top: William Clowes (1780-1851), son of a drunken potter, and co-founder of the Primitive Methodists.

Below: Hugh Bourne (1772-1852) the other founder of Primitive Methodism. He worked much of his life as a builder and carpenter, so as not to burden the church.

Methodism divided

Why did Methodism, held together so firmly under Wesley's leadership, become divided so soon after his death? Within thirty years three other Methodist churches had come into existence. The first reason was the 'clericalism' of Wesley's own type of Methodism; the second, the rigidity of its rule.

The Conference, composed exclusively of preachers, resisted any demand for the effective participation of lay people in decision-making at any level of the church's life. Decisions were made, in the last resort, by the preacher appointed to a circuit by the Conference. Laymen might suggest or argue, but they could not change policy. It was on the grounds that laymen should have real power that the first secession took place, in the North-east of England, when the Methodist New Connexion was founded in 1797.

The other two divisions occurred because 'local' preachers — lay preachers permitted to preach in the chapels of the circuit to which they belonged — broke the rules and preached beyond its boundaries, not in preaching-places or chapels, but in the open-air. Their defense was that the people to whom they preached were unchurched and had need of the gospel. They had no intention of seceding from Methodism but were excluded, ironically, for doing precisely what their founder, John Wesley, had done himself!

In the West Country the outstanding 'rebel' was a Cornishman, William O'Bryan, expelled for preaching where there were no Methodists at all, mostly in Devon. The result was the formation of the Bible Christian Church in 1815. Giving a good deal of authority to lay people, and encouraging women into the ministry, the church in its early years missioned largely in the West Country, the South of England and the Channel Islands.

The Primitive Methodists

Much the strongest and most effective of the new branches of Methodism, however, were the Primitive Methodists, formally established in 1812 after two local preachers, Hugh Bourne and William Clowes, had organized 'camp meetings' — two-day-long revival gatherings — in the Midlands, and were struck off the rolls for doing so and for continuing to preach 'where they had no right'. The name they chose indicates their belief that they were maintaining Wesley's own priorities and their constitution was traditional Methodism, though they gave a much greater share in local and connectional church government to the laity.

The Primitive Methodists found their converts where Wesley had found his, among the common people and the poor. Because of this and the social conditions of the time, they were much the most radical of all the Methodist branches, pressing for democratic reform, supporting the Chartists and, later, trades unionism. But their nickname, which they welcomed gladly, was 'the Ranters', and this they gained much more for their fervent evangelism than for their concern with human rights.

Primitive Methodism spread quickly throughout the country and by the time Hugh Bourne, an immesely able and respected leader, retired in 1842 they had a membership of 85,000.

But why was the 'breaking of rules' so harshly disciplined, especially when it was done for the sake of spreading the gospel, as the Wesleys themselves had done? Within a decade of John Wesley's death, Methodism had become increasingly bourgeois as well as firmly conservative in politics. With Napoleon threatening Britain and, at a time when any form of 'democracy' was feared as likely to bring the British government down just as the godless Revolution had done in France, Wesley's followers were anxious to be seen as a 'loyal' church and a stabilizing element in British society. They had already been attacked as possible 'enemies of the state' by leading politicians and it was not easy to defend themselves from the charge of being 'democrats' since they had effectively broken away from the state church. Demands for 'democratic reform' therefore met with rigorous opposition in the Conference, not least if they threatened the authority of the preachers.

The emergence of such apparently 'fringe groups' was probably inevitable. The tragic part of the situation was that it was in these new churches rather than in Wesley's continuing church that the true spirit of the revival was found. Wesleyan Methodism itself was in trouble.

New century

Fifty years of gain and loss: 1800-1850

Despite what they regarded as the deplorable competition from the new branches of Methodism, the Wesleyan Methodists (as they chose to call themselves) by 1825 numbered 300,000 members, four times the total at John Wesley's death. The mobility of the ministry, the use of local preachers so that all the pulpits of every circuit were filled, easy-to-understand services (though Morning Prayer was customary in the larger town chapels throughout the century) as well as its evangelical stance, all contributed to growth. The church produced leaders of notable stature and of these the most able in the first half of the new century — as well as the most notorious — was Jabez Bunting, who dominated Wesleyan Methodism in this period.

Bunting was a great preacher and administrator who, more than anyone else, encouraged the work and organisation of the Missionary Society, ensured the better training of the ministry, and committed his church to a full share in the education movement. In 1843 the Wesleyans had 31

Above: The Wesleyan chapel, Coverack, Cornwall.

Below: Queen Victoria presents a Bible.

day-schools; seven years later they had more than 700.

However, Bunting's rule had far more unhappy consequences. He was an authoritarian Tory in a church which, in contrast to other branches of Methodism, was conservative in politics and much else. The names of the huge new town-chapels — Hanover, Brunswick, Victoria — demonstrated Wesleyan loyalty to the throne. While Conference urged Wesleyan Methodists to 'Fear the Lord and the King, and meddle not with them that are given to change,' it was Jabez Bunting himself who said crisply: 'Methodism hates democracy as it hates sin.'

Bunting believed the government of the church belonged to the ordained Wesleyan ministry, and though he encouraged the use of laymen in committees, he denied them any effective access to Conference itself. (Indeed it was not until 1871, thirteen years after Bunting's death, that laymen became members of the Conference, and women were not accepted until 1910.) The result of his autocracy, however, was a growing spirit of revolt amongst a small group of ministers with inflammatory tongues and vitriolic pens who spoke for far more 'democrats' than Bunting knew existed in the church he ruled. In 1856 came the real eruption when several ministers were expelled. In that year a new denomination was formed, calling itself the United Methodist Free Churches. It was estimated that Wesleyan Methodism lost 100,000 members, though only a few joined the new church, and the majority seemed to give up church-going altogether.

The loss to the church, not only of so many members but of evangelistic zeal in exchange for an obsession for authority, is a sad commentary on a great man who in his early years did so much that was right, but in his later years believed he could do no wrong.

Vision and ventures

By mid-century the Conference's earlier warning to 'avoid those who desired change' had become meaningless. With greater stability in Britain, change had become less dangerous to the establishment. Queen Victoria was happily married and producing a large family. With 'self-help' as their inspiration, working-men climbed into the middle classes as they transformed small cottage workshops into big industrial concerns, while their work-people found long streets or back-to-back houses a vast improvement on their earlier squalid living conditions. The British Empire was annexing and 'civilizing' more and more 'primitive countries', at considerable profit to the untroubled imperialists. The Great Exhibition with its Crystal Palace, inspired by the Prince Consort, symbolized the 'new world' and while the fascinating and monstrous steam-engines on the new railways ate their way through remote rural England, writers such as Charles Dickens proved that literacy, newly gained, offered equally exciting new discoveries.

Yet in this era of change there remained tragically unchanged elements which Dickens in his serialised novels exposed below the surface of Victorian respectability — huge areas of poverty, misery and evil.

Primitive Methodists, poor themselves for the post part, had never lost sight of that half-hidden world; their passionate concern about human rights and justice stemmed from the conviction that the neglected poor were also the children of God. After 1850 the Wesleyans too turned from irrelevant debates about 'rules' and constitutions to recapture an earlier vision. They realised that there were still far too many places in Britain where there was no Methodist witness, and far too many people who had nothing to do with any church. 'Mission' began once more to come into its own — and the renewed commitment to evangelism was matched, as Wesley would have approved, by a slowly emerging passion for 'justice for the poor'.

Foreign missions continued to provide triumphant stories of advance into new areas, the conquest of cannibalism and human sacrifice (over-written but basically true), and more and more people responding to the gospel. The parallel drives of commercial imperialism and gospel grace — not so closely linked as some modern critics claim — provided familiar ground for missionary advocates and it was easy to 'raise money for missions' — at least if they were half the world away. 'Home mission' was far less exciting. One minister, however, set himself to stir the conscience of the church.

'How some of the London poor spend the night'; a contemporary illustration of the homeless in Covent Garden.

The 'Forward Movement'

Charles Prest went into action as 'Home Mission Secretary', creating a 'Forward Movement' on several fronts. It was agreed that one Sunday's collection every year should be devoted to home mission, at a time when weekly church collections had not been thought of. District missionaries were appointed to every Wesleyan district, to revive languishing chapels and to preach where there were no Methodists. Local chapels started annual 'revival campaigns', which became a normal feature throughout the country. Because the new 'watering-places' were mostly without adequate places of worship there was a campaign to raise money for new chapels and ministry at seaside resorts. An experiment of providing clergy for the army in the Crimea led to the establishment of chaplaincy services in the army and soon afterwards in the navy.

Nothing is further from the truth than our nostalgic assumption that in 'the good old days' everyone went to church. Most people never went near it, apart from marriages and funerals. The poor — sadly accurate — thought respectable church-goers had no place for them and it was this that led a Wesleyan minister to begin one of the world's most famous organisations. To us it is unthinkable that one had to pay to get the best seats in a Wesleyan chapel! Not that one paid at the door, but most seats in most chapels were rented to 'pew-holders'. When William Booth then a young minister in Nottingham, led a group of ill-dressed poor people to a Wesley chapel they were turned away and told they might find some seats behind the pulpit. Angry and disillusioned, Booth left the Wesleyan ministry and started the Salvation Army, to concentrate his efforts on those who saw no hope and had no place in contemporary organized church-life.

City campaigners

Two other Wesleyan ministers stand out as men who acted on the belief that the gospel of Jesus Christ is relevant to every part of life — T. B. Stephenson and Hugh Price Hughes.

Thomas Bowman Stephenson was appointed to Lambeth and, like most men sent to work in inner London, was appalled by what he found. The police brought to his notice the shocking conditions of boys and girls who were completely homeless. Walking one night with Francis Horner, a young man who was to be one of his closest collaborators, a policeman showed them a litter of boxes and tarpaulins — the very place for rats and vermin. Shining his bull's-eye lantern, the policeman gave a shout and out from under the rotten covering swarmed a score of ragged, shivering, filthy boys. Stephenson and his friend were immediately driven to action. He hired a disused donkey-stable and, after cleaning it up, took two boys to live in it. That was the beginning of more than a century of inspired child-care — The National Children's Home. To look after the children he selected young women for training as 'sisters', a life-vocation, and in this way began a corps of skilled and dedicated women who were to serve the church in Britain and overseas with great devotion and distinction — the Methodist Deaconess Order.

Hugh Price Hughes (1847-1902); the central halls and city missions of British Methodism are his lasting memorial.

Hugh Price Hughes engaged in no such dramatic programmes, but he was undoubtedly the dominant figure in the Wesleyan ministry, as well known outside as inside the church. When the playwrights Ibsen and G.B. Shaw were vilified for exposing the evils of society, men such as Hughes were also beginning to stir the conscience of the church about injustice and vice. Stationed in the West London Mission, Hughes's headquarters in St. James's Hall in Piccadilly became the center of the 'Forward Movement' initiated by Charles Prest. Conservatism had lost ground in Wesleyan Methodism since the mid-century and the majority of Methodists who were politically aware were supporters of the new 'Liberal' party, which saw relgion, politics and social affairs as being irrevocably inter-related. Hughes became their acknowledged leader.

Hughes founded *The Methodist Times,* at a period when other religious papers were careful to keep clear of 'radical' politics, to probe the ethical aspects of every social issue of the time. In his afternoon meetings at St. James's Hall he never hesitated to discuss such topics as 'Christ and Poverty' or 'Christ and the Music-Hall'. Neither urbane nor polished in his speech, his oratory was unrestrained, fiery Welsh passion. Without the time to engage in 'reforms' himself, he incessantly urged the need for them — as, for instance, in a series of lectures on the London County Council where he discussed public markets, gas, municipal docks, the poor law, the police and much else.

Because he recognized that there was little that really divided non-Roman, non-Anglican churches, he was an early advocate of Methodist reunion and, in 1896, co-founded with Sidney Berry the Free Church Council.

The mission to the poor

Hughes was the spokesman for other men. The first 'city mission' in Methodism was begun in Liverpool in 1865 by Charles Garrett, but Manchester and London provide the most vivid examples of Methodism's 'mission to the poor' in the great cities. In Manchester Samuel Collier captured the public ear, transferring his Sunday evening preaching-service to the Free Trade Hall, which he filled every week for more than twenty years. The

Mission itself not only had open-air work and lodging-house services, but it ran a men's home, a labor yard for the unemployed and a medical centre. In much the same way Thomas Jackson matched evangelism and social action in London. He was a Primitive Methodist minister appointed to Whitechapel in London, and found no members at all on his church-roll. Within a year he had 90 members and had already begun a remarkable service to the poor of the East End, with his soup kitchen, free breakfasts for poor children, labor bureau for the unemployed, medical mission and homeless lads' institute specialising in rehabilitating 'first offenders'.

These activities were followed by the opening of 'central halls' in all the bigger towns of Britain, and eventually by the erection of the magnificent Westminster Central Hall in 1912.

Fathers of chapels

For most of the nineteenth century a few courageous Methodists were also engaged in a very different kind of political activity.

Three of the six farm-laborers who tried to found the first effective agricultural trade-union were local preachers at a time when the Wesleyans were hide-bound anti-democrats. When these history-making 'Tolpuddle martyrs' were transported for life, the Wesleyan Conference neither protested nor helped them or their families.

Primitive Methodists were very different. They were active in Trade Unions almost from their legal foundation in 1825. Many of their members worked in the mills, on the land, in the factories and the mines, and they knew at first hand how men and women, and even children, had to labor for long hours in appalling conditions for desperately low pay. Active in their local chapels they were accustomed to 'speaking out' and to organizing in groups. Not surprisingly therefore the early trade unions were often set up along 'chapel lines', beginning with prayer and taking weekly payments from members already accustomed to the idea of weekly class-money. Indeed, the name 'chapel' still survives in some cases, as the name for trade union branch meetings.

Two Primitive Methodist Trade Unionists deserve to be specially remembered. Joseph Arch had a particularly difficult time persuading farm-laborers to forget their isolation and put aside their traditional apathy and hopelessness. Yet he became the one man above all others who gained better wages and working-conditions for farm-workers, and in addition helped over half a million to find a new life through emigration.

Peter Lee, a pit boy when he was nine, is more securely remembered. He emigrated twice, to America and South Africa, but returned to mining in the North-East. Over the years he became both a leader in the Miners' Association and the Chairman of Durham County Council. Preaching on Sundays and Union work during the week were his life's work, and he was fittingly commemorated when the government gave one of the new towns, in County Durham, the name of Peterlee.

Westminster Central Hall, opened in 1912.

America

American Methodism

No book dealing with Methodism can omit the fact that there are fifteen million members in the United States Methodist churches — even if many of them do not know that their founder, Francis Asbury, was a Methodist preacher sent to pre-Revolutionary America by John Wesley in 1771.

Severed from Britain at the end of the War of Independence and rejoicing in the ordination of Francis Asbury by Thomas Coke in 1784, American Methodism immediately began its own independent existence. When, in the absence of any Anglican clergy, Asbury took the title of 'bishop' instead of 'superintendent', the church took the title of the Methodist Episcopal Church of America, with Asbury as its leader and inspiration. While the statue of John Wesley outside the New Room in Bristol shows a trim figure sitting easily in the saddle, that of Asbury, in Washington, is of an almost exhausted rider, frontiersman's hat dangling from his hand, on an equally tired horse. No man rode farther in almost impossible condition than he did, and all in the name of Christ.

Asbury was, nevertheless, only one rider among many. Though British circuits were large by our standards, American circuits were immense and the 'circuit riders' between them covered the whole country, including California before it became one of the American states. Their courage and their faith were stupendous, and they won great victories both in settled communities and among the westward-trekking pioneers. Until the 1840s Methodism was dedicated to an evangelical mission to the nation and its membership and influence grew year by year. Then came the disastrous year, 1844.

In theory Methodism had from the beginning been opposed to slavery, but in the southern states, which depended on Negro slave-labor in the cotton-fields, there were many slave-owning Methodist

The first Methodist sermon in Baltimore, Maryland.

families and even a slave-owning bishop. It was he who was made a test-case by the northern reformers in the 1844 Conference, and the result of bitter and extended debates was the division of Methodism into the Methodist Episcopal Church and the Methodist Episcopal Church South. Not until 1939 were they reunited under the simpler name of 'The Methodist Church'. But the Civil War also resulted, after the end of slavery, in the creation of three other separate, and very strong, black churches. Constantly expanding all over the nation in the following years, Methodism − or at least white Methodism − was to share in the growing affluence of the United States and to a limited measure from the swelling tide of European immigrants.

Today, British visitors to the USA may be surprised at the size and extent of church premises. Closer inquiry leaves them even more surprised by the strength and variety of church-based educational programmes, the study and fellowship groups which meet at an hour in the morning unthinkable in Britain, and the church's commitment to 'social mission'. The reputation of the large Methodist hospitals, for instance, the quality of life in its homes for the elderly and the imaginative provision of large 'retirement communities' are proof that affluence, responsibly used with typical American initiative, can contribute greatly to human betterment. True it is a middle-class church with few racially-integrated congregations, but British Methodism can hardly, in general, claim any different situation.

The First Methodist Church, Albuquerque, New Mexico. The Methodist church is today very strong in North America.

A statuette of one of Wesley's North American 'circuit riders'.

Unity

American Mission

There are, however, two particular areas in which American Methodism can claim very significant achievements. As in Britain, mission to the rest of the world only followed after a long period of consolidation at home. The first missions were to the American Indians but, by the second half of the century, especially under the inspiration and example of the indefatigable William Taylor, they had encompassed the world. Taylor travelled very widely – in India, Ceylon, Southern Asia and Australasia, in South Africa and South America – and everywhere he attempted to follow the same pattern. In each case he stayed in the area for a considerable period, conducting missions, often to the educated or to those who spoke English. Ideally, and often in fact, this became the base for the work of the resident American missionaries. Taylor attempted to ensure self-support by starting fee-paying schools. Though his success varied, his enthusiasm and his speaking tours across the USA helped to set the church on fire for mission across the world.

At home the most far-reaching contribution was in education. Because religion may not be taught in state schools the churches developed very comprehensive weekly religious educational programmes as part of their life. But Methodist involvement in education went very much further than this, and it is claimed that at

least a third of the colleges and universities in the USA can be traced to a Methodist foundation.

Methodist union

There had been talk of Methodist reunion in Britain long before the end of the century, but it was not until 1907 that the first union took place. Even then the two largest churches remained outside, but the Methodist New Connexion, the Bible Christians and the United Methodist Free Churches came together with the slightly misleading name of the 'United Methodist Church'. There were many, however, who planned and worked for wider union and, though World War I diverted thought and energies from structural questions, Methodist Union was eventually achieved in 1932. 'The Methodist Church' was reborn and though in many villages and small towns, in particular, old rivalries and folk-memories did not die until a whole

generation had died, too, the union was successful.

To this renewed Church the Wesleyan Methodists brought 539,000 members, the Primitive Methodists 206,000 and the United Methodists 159,000. But membership was already declining and, despite unrealistic hopes, union did not bring revival. World War I had had a disastrous effect on faith and morals and helped to spread a shallow materialism; and World War II, so soon after Union, left blitzed church premises, massive shifts in population, and a further decline in ethical standards, Christian certainty and religious habits.

Today Methodist membership in Britain is only half of what it was in 1932. Depressing though this is, critics outside the churches and defeatists inside have consistently prophesied the quick and certain demise of the church as a whole, for what has happened in Methodism has been

Revd. Dr. Kenneth Greet, until recently President of the Methodist Conference.

Lord Soper, who has become world-famous for his uncompromising preaching at Tower Hill and Speakers' Corner.

matched in all the historic churches not only in Britain but also in continental Europe.

Yet, despite the recession in church-membership, Methodism in Britain over the past thirty years has shown vitality in its leadership, openness to ecumenical life and imaginative commitment to service. Like almost all non-fundamentalist churches, its failure has been to discover a vital and effective form of evangelism which would match Wesley's missionary activity two centuries ago. Despite this, the Methodist Church still continues to make a significant contribution to life.

Giants of the pulpit

Every generation has its giants and three men, all contemporaries, towered high above most church leaders in Britain — Leslie Weatherhead, W. E. Sangster and Donald Soper. All were brilliant speakers from pulpit and platform, all were best-selling writers and all drew large numbers of people to a new understanding of the faith and to an experience of Christ.

Leslie Weatherhead, gentle and persuasive in presenting the 'transforming friendship' of Jesus, was an outstanding pioneer in psychological counselling from a religious base, to which he gave a great deal of his time.

W. E. Sangster was the evanglist par excellence, an incomparable preacher whose unrestrained London accent became as familiar in America or Australia as in Britain. His books were aimed at

An evangelist at work in contemporary Africa.

personal and church renewal and he held great crowds wherever he spoke, particularly during his outstanding ministry at Westminster Central Hall. His famous New Year sermon on social evils made headlines in all the media, and his early death was an irreparable loss to Christian leadership in church and nation.

Donald Soper, given a seat in the House of Lords, where he makes an authoritative contribution, has been Methodism's outstanding 'prophet' since he began open-air speaking at Tower Hill and Hyde Park Corner in the 1920s, a practice he still continues every week with consummate skill. As an unshakeable pacifist and socialist, he has always refused to divorce politics and religion.

World War II and after

In a very different way Douglas Griffiths left a remarkable legacy because of his understanding of young people. Working with them in the war, 'Griff' founded the Methodist Association of Youth Clubs, and since the 1940s MAYC has brought innumerable young people into the church and to dedicated service in secular life. Though youth club programmes change with the years, 'Griff's' standards are still central to the best of them.

Ministers may make a name for themselves in Christian circles, but laymen can make a wide impact which few ministers can match. To take an example from political life, it is remarkable that three successive Speakers of the House of Commons have been Methodists, and the last, George Thomas, a miner's son now ennobled as Viscount Tonypandy, has been hailed as one of the greatest Speakers in the last three centuries of Parliament. He never failed to witness with impressive conviction to his Christian faith, which gave point to all he did, and still does.

During the years since World War II the ministry has changed in several ways. Older candidates are now readily accepted, bringing the experience of long years of secular life. More dramatically it was decided in 1973 to accept women into the ministry – a long-delayed response to a proposal first made to the Wesleyan Conference in 1926. It may continue to make union with the Church of England more difficult, but in any case, unhappily, the scheme for Anglican-Methodist unity, on which so many in both churches placed high hopes was in 1969 rejected by the Church of England, though it was accepted by the Methodist Conference. That failure to move to corporate integration, however, has not inhibited local schemes of ecumenical co-operation. These include jointly-planned action, joint services of confirmation, united worship and shared buildings, which are often used by other churches besides Methodists and Anglicans.

Methodism has also made notable responses to such social changes as the new multi-racial society and the ageing population. While the Notting Hill Carnival is regularly featured on TV, for instance, with its emphasis on multi-racial harmony in public enjoyment, few people know of the imaginative and constructive work of Notting Hill Methodist Church, in which even deeper multi-racial relationships are formed and sustained with real effect on the life of the neighborhood. And though there are too few such outstanding contributions in the churches of our inner cities, this is by no means a sole example.

Probably, however, the outstanding social contribution of Methodism in post-war years, matching the founding of the National Children's Home a century ago, has been through the Methodist Homes for the Aged. Begun in the most desperate years of World War II, in 1943, this visionary service for the elderly now has 1,000 residents in 35 homes in every part of Britain. It is doubling that caring capacity in the present decade through its entry into 'sheltered housing'.

'Alongside the poor'

It is true that Methodist life today is at its strongest in 'outer city suburbia' and that, with the rest of society, it has largely withdrawn from the old concentrations in the inner cities. But to read through three or four issues of the *Methodist Recorder*, the independent weekly started in 1861, is to gain a realistic view of what is happening in the church which John Wesley began with his field-preaching in Bristol so long ago. Every week there is news of new or redeveloped churches in town and country, of young people in community action, of members added to the church, of evangelistic enterprise in many forms. Some people *are* deliberately moving back into city centers as a way of Christian witness,

Pupils at the Hairrampur School for the Poor.

and the Conference's acceptance of 'mission alongside the poor' as a priority task of the church may lead to a rediscovery of Wesley's own estimate of the poor as the people for whom Jesus had a special love.

Over 30,000 new members were added to the Methodist Church in Britain between 1980-83. True, almost the same number died, so there are not sufficient new members to tilt the balance of gain and loss. But people, especially young people, do not normally choose to link themselves in such numbers to a dull, unattractive ineffective or expiring church.

The Church in Europe, whatever section of it we look at, is struggling — not to survive, but to find ways of making an effective witness in a chaos of political conflict, protests against nuclear arms and fear of a nuclear holocaust, crass materialism and escapism in bizarre and sometimes horrific forms. Methodism shares in that struggle. But to gain a true perspective of the life of contemporary Methodism we need to look beyond ourselves and our European counterparts. We need to lift our eyes to the world.

Wesley's world parish

Within a few decades of Thomas Coke's death on the way to Ceylon, Methodism was at work in five continents. Divided though it was, it shared the same vision of a world won for Christ. Nor did one part of Methodism compete with another in its overseas enterprise. Primitive Methodist missionaries went to Nigeria and Rhodesia; the United Methodist Free Churches to Sierra Leone. The Bible Christians pioneered in China, and so did all the other branches of Methodism, but each of them in different parts of that vast region. It was in China that medical missions were first begun. Women were an organised part of Methodism's missionary work from 1858.

Some of the work was unrewarding, all of it was hard, occasionally it was dangerous, and especially in West Africa a missionary knew he was likely to be dead in a year or so and often within months. But there were great triumphs, too. The islands of the Pacific, with a tradition of cannibalism, had turned to Christ by the middle of the nineteenth century. So had the Maoris of New Zealand. Parts of West Africa responded to the gospel with joyous acceptance, and there were notable mass-movemovements in India, South-west China and the Ivory Coast around the beginning of the present century.

From that time, too, national leadership came to the fore largely because of the emphasis on Christian education. There was a steady development from 'mission' to 'church'. Then, from the 1960s, came an even more significant development. In the post-war world, where western imperialism gave way to the creation of new national states, there came a parallel change in the church's status. Encouraged by the Methodist Church in Britain the old 'districts' directed by the Missionary Society in London became 'autonomous churches' with their own national leadership within self-governing Conferences.

Many of the autonomous Conferences, still needing and welcoming missionaries from Britain, nevertheless began to exchange personnel with other Methodist Churches — the Caribbean, for instance, provided some essential leadership in West Africa; Papua New Guinea sent its own missionaries, by invitation, to work in Indonesia and in aboriginal mission in Australia. Many of the most inspiring leaders in the world church came from the Third World. Methodists such as D. T. Niles of Ceylon and Philip Potter, West Indian General Secretary of the World Council of Churches, had an incalculable influence on the thinking of Christians of every church all over the world.

Christian unity

The most dramatic and challenging advance in Christian Unity came from what, not many decades before, had been very much a 'missionary church', with the creation in 1946 of the Church of South India; a union of Anglicans, Methodists, Congregationalists and Presbyterians. Methodism has rejoiced to lose its own identity in a church which proves that 'unity works' and can achieve a strength of witness and action impossible to those who are divided.

Boundaries are being crossed, too, in the opposite direction as British Methodism, in common with all the major denominations, brings overseas ministers to work for a period of years in British circuit life, or challenges the home church with short visits by ministers and lay people, both men and women, in its 'Mission to Britain' programme.

But these are fairly limited examples chosen only from *British* Methodism's links with the world church. Apart from the preponderant American scene, the Methodist Church of Australasia and South Africa have been engaged in mission and evangelism through the long years of their existence. American Methodism in particular has been responsible for far vaster areas of mission than anywhere else.

The statistics of World Methodism are revealing:

Africa 2,658,199 members
Asia 3,568,986 members
Central and South America and the Caribbean 517,846 members
Europe 749,090 members
The Pacific 941,790 members
North America 15,242,564 members

In total, World Methodism has 23,595,476 members, and a Methodist Community of 51,736,569. And the number grows every year.

Today, Wesley's world parish is something he could not even have dreamed of. It must remain committed to the joyous task about which Charles Wesley sang:

What we have felt and seen,
With confidence we tell;
And publish to the sons of men
The signs infallible.

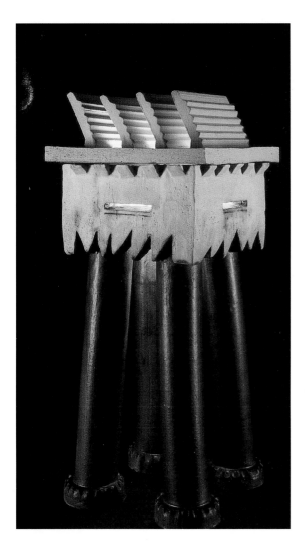

OLIVIER ROLLIN
*Four Legged
Lamp, 1996*
*16" x 6" x 6" (40 x
15 x 15 cm)*
*Handbuilt clay, legs
extruded*
PHOTO BY ARTIST

**ROD
MCCORMICK**
Nantes, 1989
*38" x 12" x 12"
(95 x 30 x 30 cm)*
*Welded and
formed steel,
brass, aluminum*
PHOTO BY ARTIST

GARRY KNOX BENNETT
From "Lamps, 1990-91"
24" x 8" (60 x 20 cm)
Plastic tubing, sheet metal, wood
PHOTO BY JUDY REED

Kim Kelzer
Pumpkin Pair, 1997
32" x 7" x 7" (80 x 17.5 x 17.5 cm)
Painted wood, lead, cherry wood,
and paper over old bedsprings

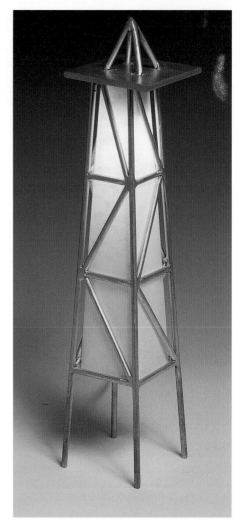

Chris Darway
Diver Lamp, 1992
14" x 8" x 9"
(35 x 20 x 22.5 cm)
Bronze, copper, cast resin knob,
Plexiglass

Christopher Anna
Oil Lamp, 1997
18" x 4" x 4" (45 x 10 x
10 cm)
Steel and paper

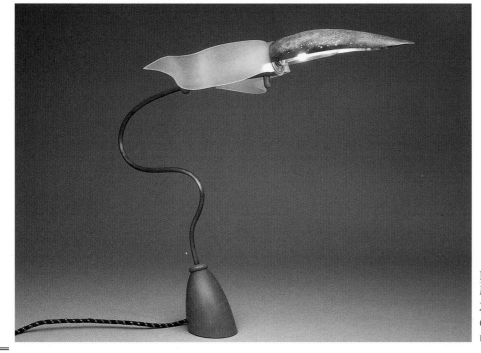

Kim Kelzer
Desk Lamp, 1990
24" x 20" (60 x 50 cm)
Cherry wood, copper, Plexiglass

RICHARD KOOYMAN AND BARBARA BROWNING
Table Lamp, 1996
36" tall (90 cm)
Wood, aluminum, paint
PHOTO BY JERRY ANTHONY

GARRY KNOX BENNETT
9 Inch Drawer Lamp, 1994
72-1/2" x 24" x 17-1/2" (181 x 60 x 44 cm)
Wood, metal, paper
PHOTO BY F. LEE FATHEREE

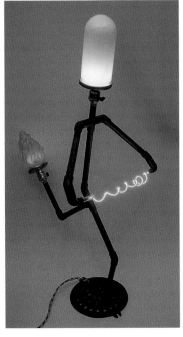

HARRY ANDERSON
Prometheus, 1983
42" x 21" x 25" (105 x 52.5 x 62.5 cm)
Plastic, glass, neon
PHOTO BY ARTIST

HARRY ANDERSON
Totem Series, 1988
left: 30" x 6" x 6" (75 x 15 x 15 cm), right: 28" x 7" x 7" (70 x 17.5 x 17.5 cm)
Found objects, iron, glass
PHOTO BY ARTIST

135

MARY GINN
Arete, 1997
22" x 16" (55 x 40 cm)
Galvanized wire, Kozo (paper mulberry), ceramic base (cone 6 red clay, cone 6 oxidation semi-gloss black)

KIM KELZER
Burning Toast Nite Light, 1997
16" x 14" x 8" (40 x 35 x 20 cm)
Toaster, painted wood, flicker flame bulbs

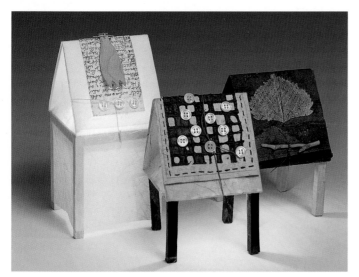

CLAUDIA LEE
untitled, 1998
7-3/4" x 4" x 4" (19 x 10 x 10 cm) and 6-1/2" x 4" x 4" (16 x 10 x 10 cm)
Purchased and handmade papers, found objects, wooden forks, handstitching

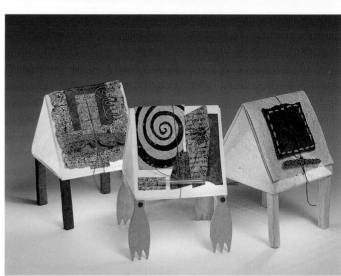

CLAUDIA LEE
untitled, 1998
6-1/2" x 4" x 4" (16 x 10 x 10 cm)
Purchased and handmade papers, found objects, wooden forks, handstitching

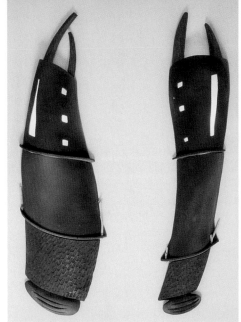

KATHY TRIPLETT
untitled, 1997
5' x 14" (1.5 m x 35 cm)
Clay (cone 3) and glass
PHOTO BY ARTIST

NEIL BENSON
from left to right:
Clown Toy Lamp, 1996
6' tall (1.8 m)
Found toys
Popcorn Lamp 1, 1996
6' tall (1.8 m)
Found toys
Gloria Webb Lamp, 1997
6' tall (1.8 m)
*Found objects from the
Webb's trash*
PHOTO BY ARTIST

RICK MELBY
*Post-Apocalypse
Torchiére, 1988*
*82" tall x 14" diame-
ter (205 x 35 cm)*
*Found objects, glass
rods, painted wood,
copper tubing*
PHOTO BY JORGÉ ALVAREZ

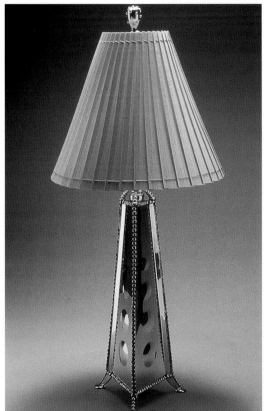

LEON FONTIER
Buffet Lamp, 1994
22" high (55 cm)
*Lead-free pewter with
bright finish*
Lamp shade by John Lang
PHOTO BY BRANTLEY CARROLL

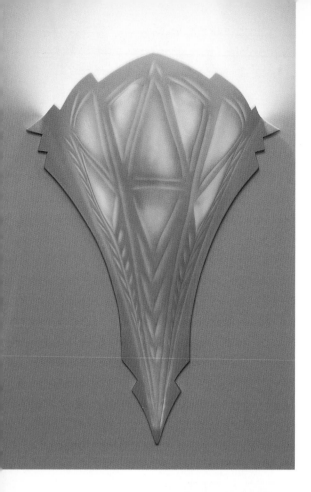

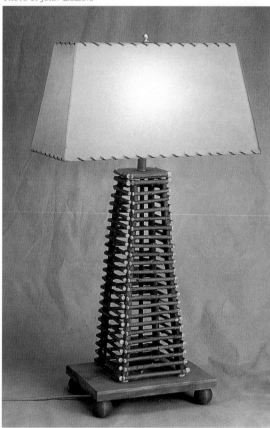

**AMY SARNER
WILLIAMS**
Wall Torch, 1993
13" x 9" x 3-1/2"
(32.5 x 22.5 x 9 cm)
Translucent porcelain
PHOTO BY JOHN CARLANO

JERRY WOMACKS
*Oil Rig Table Lamp,
1995*
29" tall (72.5 cm)
*Cherry base, maple ball
feet, willow twigs,
parchment shade,
rawhide lacing*
PHOTO BY JERRY ANTHONY

KATHY TRIPLETT
untitled, 1997
18" x 10" (45 x 25 cm)
Clay (cone 3) and glass
PHOTO BY TIM BARNSWELL

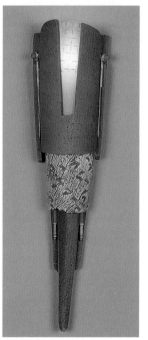

DON DAVIS
untitled, 1995
24" tall
*Thrown porcelain clay with oxide
sprays and glaze trailing*
PHOTO BY TIM BARNWELL

ROD McCORMICK
Infundibulum, 1996
36" x 20" x 18" (90 x 50 x 45 cm)
Welded and formed steel
PHOTO BY ARTIST

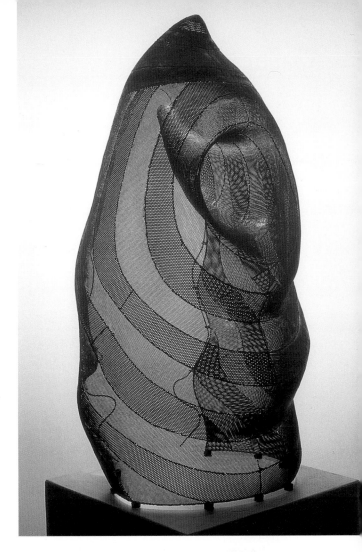

OLIVIER ROLLIN
Tree Lamp, 1996
18" tall x 12" diameter (45 x 30 cm)
Clay base with shade made from slumped glass, arranged and fused
PHOTO BY ARTIST

SUE JOHNSON
untitled, 1992
20" x 17" (50 x 42.5 cm)
Found object (oxidized, brass shell casing), copper-plated eucalyptus leaf, mica, laminated natural eucalyptus leaves
PHOTO BY CARL NELSON

SUE JOHNSON
untitled, 1994
28" x 21" (70 x 52.5 cm)
West Coast Myrtle Burl, mica shade, design on parchment
PHOTO BY CARL NELSON

Gallery Designers

HARRY ANDERSON
6805 N. 12Th Street
Philadelphia, PA 19126
(215) 548-8074
Contemporary artist Harry Anderson creates illuminated sculptures from found objects. His work has been widely exhibited and is included in many public and private collections. It is available through the Snyderman Gallery in Philadelphia, The Glass Gallery in Bethesda, Maryland, and The Wetsman Collection in Birmingham, Michigan.

CHRISTOPHER ANNA
817 West End Avenue, #1A
New York, NY 10025
(212) 864-9128
Christopher Anna designs and creates furniture in his Brooklyn studio. He lives in New York City and can be reached at (212) 864-9128.

GARRY KNOX BENNETT
1011 Grand Street
Alameda, CA 94501
(510) 522-6450
Gary Knox Bennett is an artist who is primarily known for his furniture, lamps, and clocks. His works are presently on exhibit with the Leo Kaplan Moderne Gallery in New York City.

NEIL BENSON
111 N. Mole Street
Philadelphia, PA 19102
(215) 963-9850
Neil Benson, a photojournalist since 1970, has worked for People Magazine *and the* New York Times. *Co-Founder of Philadelphia's Dumpster Divers in the early 1990's, he currently makes lamps, jewelry, and sculpture from found objects. "Every day the city puts treasures at the curbside—I just have to go find them." He cites the dumpster diver motto, "Ejectamentum Nummi Nostrum—Your Trash is Our Cash."*

CHRISTOPHER DARWAY
1 Feeder Street
Lambertville, NJ 08530
(609) 397-9550
<darwaydesign@juno.com>
Metalwork in the form of lamps, jewelry, and hamster traps keeps Mr. Darway, a metals teacher, busy in his Lambertville, New Jersey studio, located on the banks of the Delaware River.

DON DAVIS
Asheville, NC 28804
Don Davis has been working as a studio potter in Asheville, North Carolina since 1976. He is the author of another recently published book, Wheel-Thrown Ceramics: Altering, Trimming, Adding, Finishing *(Lark,1998)*

LEON FONTIER
Fontier Designs
1405 Woodhull Road
Troupsburg, NY 14885
(607) 525-6135
Leon Fontier designs and produces his pewterware, using a variety of techniques, in his studio in Troupsburg, New York. His work is part of the permanent collection of the Yale University Art Gallery, the White House Collection, and many private collections. His work is shown at major galleries and craft shows throughout the United States and Canada.

MARY GINN
Firefly Design
20415 80th Avenue, NE
Bothell, WA 98011
Mary Ginn has spent the last ten years studying and making paper, five of which she spent in Japan. The Japanese style of papermaking is a steady influence on her artistic creations. "In my mind, the organic process of Japanese papermaking lends itself beautifully to the organic shapes I produce." She may be contacted at Firefly Design, Bothell, WA or e-mail her at <bginn@gte.net>.

SUE JOHNSON
Sue Johnson Custom Lamps & Shades
1745 Solano Avenue
Berkeley, CA 94707
(510) 527-2623
Sue Johnson has spent the past 25 years exploring her fascination with light and textures through her business Sue Johnson Custom Lamps & Shades. Sue is personally drawn to handmade and functional objects. "I encourage everyone to search their houses for hidden personal treasures that would come to life by being incorporated in a lamp, and every time that lamp is lit, a personal memory will be rekindled."

KIM KELZER
P.O. Box 1372
Freeland, WA 98249
(360) 331-2795
Kimster@whidbey.com
Kim Kelzer creates one of a kind lamps and furniture in her studio in Washington. She shows her work in galleries throughout the country including Ter Cera Gallery, Palo Alto and Los Gatos, California; Gallery Naga, Boston, Massachusetts; John Elder Gallery, New York, New York.

RICHARD KOOYMAN AND BARBARA BROWNING
P.O. Box 2248
Frankfort, MI 49635
RKMAN@BENZIE.com
Kooyman and Browning construct one-of-a-kind objects incorporating figurative and animal imagery.

CLAUDIA LEE
Claudia Lee Studios
317 Cumberland Street
Kingsport, TN 37660-4401
(423) 378-4933
Claudia Lee is a full-time paper artist and bookbinder. She travels to workshops around the United States to share her knowledge and skills with others.

ROD McCORMICK
P.O. Box 29578
Philadelphia. PA 19144
(215) 843-9866
Rod McCormick teaches jewelry, metalsmithing, and metal furniture at The University of the Arts in Philadelphia. His work is represented by the John Elder Gallery, New York, New York.

RICK MELBY
37 Biltmore Avenue
Asheville, NC 28801
(828) 232-0905
Rick Melby's work has been exhibited and collected internationally. He currently lives and works in Asheville, North Carolina.

Acknowledgments

OLIVIER ROLLIN
Asheville, NC 28801
Olivier Rollin is a French multimedia artist, formally trained in industrial design, who now resides in Asheville, North Carolina. "In my designs, a lamp is not necessarily separated into a shade and a base. They are one, and together they work like a piece of sculpture."

KATHY TRIPLETT
Weaverville, NC 28787
Kathy Triplett has worked primarily with clay for the past 28 years, creating wall pieces, tiles, and sculptural teapots. She values lighting fixtures as functional forms of her sculpture. She is the author of Handbuilt Ceramics *(Lark, 1997).*

AMY SARNER WILLIAMS
1122 S. 48Th Street
Philadelphia, PA 19143
(215) 724-7348
(215) 925-7774 fax
Amy Sarner Williams creates lighting for the spirit as well as the senses. Her translucent porcelain "wall torches" emit a warm luminescence.

JERRY WOMACKS
Womacks Studio
114 Woodrow Street
Yellow Springs, OH 45387
(937) 767-1720
<jwomax@aol.com>
Jerry Womacks and his wife Paula have been designing and building furniture and accessories since 1976. "Our interest in rustic twig work began in 1994 when our family bought a cabin in Minnesota. Twig work is a very free and playful medium to work in and always fun to live around."

KYLE SPENCER
is a glass artist and sculptor who also designs lamps. A fine arts graduate of the University of Michigan, he also studied at the Penland School in North Carolina. Spencer said the transition to lamp design was an easy one because he already was using light as a medium in his sculptures.

This book would not have been possible without the talent and time of the designers who created these extraordinary lamps. Many of these designers have contributed numerous projects for numerous Lark Books (you know who you are!) and we are forever grateful. To the new designers, we express our thanks, and we hope that this is the beginning of an enduring relationship.

A special thanks to Ronnie Meyers of Magnolia Beauregard's Antiques, Craig Culbertson and Otto Hauser of Stuf Antiques, and Linda Constable at Sluder's Furniture, Asheville businesses that loaned us props. Thank you Otto for being so patient and thorough during the how-to photography session: you are a star!

Thank you Scott Kenyon and The Lamp Shop for loaning us the lamp shade parts.

Thank you, thank you to Diane and Dick Weaver, Ronnie Meyers, Olivier Rollin, Shelley Lowell, Terry Taylor, and Jeff Webb for allowing us to make use of their fabulous homes for the location photography.

Last, but certainly not least, a round of applause for Richard Babb for his elegant photography.

Sources for Lampmaking Supplies

Parts, Bases, and Shades

DELPHI STAINED GLASS
3380 East Jolly Road
Lansing, MI 48910
(800) 248-2048
http://www.delphiglass.com
Lamp bases, materials for crafting glass shades, tools, and some electrical components

ELECTRICAL CONNECTIONS, INC.
3704 Friendsview Drive
Greensboro, NC 27410
(800) 741-7329
Lamp parts and electrical components, including, sockets, cord sets, and bulbs

HERALD'S LAMP
1912 N. 45th Street
Seattle, WA 98103
(800) 779-2558
Manufacturer, wholesaler and retailer of lamp parts, bases, shades, and electrical components. Call for specific parts or advice. No catalog.

LAMP SPECIALTIES
Box 240
Westville, NJ 08093-0240
(800) 225-5526
http://www.lamp-specialties.com
Lamp parts, shade materials, and kits

MAINELY SHADES
100 Gray Road
Falmouth, ME 04105
(800) 624-6359
http://www.mainelyshades.com
Lamp shade frames, shade materials, lamp bases, components, books, and kits. Check out their informative website for products and advice for lampmaking projects.

MUNRO CRAFTS
3954 West 12 Mile Road
Berkeley, MI 48072
(800) 638-0543
Electrical components and wiring, shade parts, adhesive shades, linen shades for painting, glass paint, some kits and books

NATIONAL ARTCRAFT COMPANY
7996 Darrow Road
Twinsburg, OH 44087
(888) 937-2723 for orders only
(800) 526-7419 other inquiries
http://www.nationalartcraft.com
Lighting and electrical components, bulbs, bases, shades, kits, plus art supplies

PARTS-4-LAMPS
4746 Plymouth Lane
Lakeland, FL 33810
(910) 815-7294
http://www.wbus.com/parts4lamps
Good source for lamp parts when you are restoring an old lamp or need an unusual piece. The on-line catalog features over one thousand parts and includes lamp bases, shades, and electrical components.

THE LAMP SHOP
P.O. Box 3606
Concord, NH 03302-3606
(603) 224-1603
Lampmaking supplies, including, shade materials and frames, bases, electrical components, tools, books, and kits. Will special order for hard-to-find items.

Speciality Lamp Shade Materials

ANTIQUE LAMP SHADE FRAME COMPANY
4275 Southwest 185th
Aloha, OR 97007
(503) 642-7725
e-mail: bcooper863@aol.com
Custom-designed wire frames for lamp shades. Send a photo of the shade you want to make and the owner will craft a wire frame to match.

DANIEL SMITH, INC.
4150 1st Avenue S
P.O. Box 84268
Seattle, WA 98124
(800) 426-6740
Full line of art supplies and papers. Good selection of unusual handmade papers for decorating that special lamp shade.

HOLLYWOOD LIGHTS
800 Wisconsin Street, Suite D02-104
Eau Claire, WI 54703-3598
(715) 834-8707
Manufacturer of self-adhesive luminator lamp kits and other paper shade products. Check with your local craft dealer or call direct for a retail distributor in your area.

PEARL PAINT
308 Canal Street
New York City, NY 10013
(800) 221-6845
http://www.pearlpaint.com
Extensive assortment of rare papers. Huge selection of fine arts and craft supplies from around the world at discounted prices. Pearl will special order items to meet your needs, and welcomes international orders.

TARHEEL MICA COMPANY, INC.
P.O. Box 8, Highway 19E
Plumtree, NC 28664
(704) 765-4535
Sheets of mica; some custom lamp components

Baskets and Gourds

H.H. PERKINS COMPANY
10 S. Bradley Road
Woodbridge, CT 06525
(203) 389-9501
Wholesale and retail basketry materials and books

OZARK COUNTRY CREATIONS
30226 Holly Road
Pierce City, MO 65723
(417) 476-5454
Craft-ready gourds

PURPLE MARTIN CONSERVATION ASSOCIATION
Edinboro University of Pennsylvania
Edinboro, PA 16444
(814) 734-4420
http://www.purplemartin.org
Gourds sold in packs starting at $24.95, plus shipping and handling. Use extra gourds for birdhouses. Profits go to help fund research and conservation for purple martins.

ROYALWOOD LTD.
517 Woodville Road
Mansfield, OH 44907
(419) 526-1630
Basketry materials, tools, and books

THE BASKET MAKER'S CATALOG
GH Productions
521 E. Walnut Street
Dept. EM
Scottsville, KY 42164
(800) 447-7008
http://www.basketmakerscatalog.com/
Basketry materials, tools, dyes, and kits

THE CANING SHOP
926 Gilman Street
Berkeley, CA 94710
(800) 544-3373
Owned by the co-author of The Complete Book of Gourd Craft and author of The Caner's Handbook. Basketry materials, tools, and books

THE GOURD FACTORY
P.O. Box 9
Linden, CA 95236
(209) 887-3694
http://home.inreach.com/~gourdfac/index.html
Craft-ready gourds. Minimum order of $50.

THE GOURD FARM
Route 1, Box 73
Wrens, GA 30833
(706) 547-6784
Craft-ready gourds

WEST MOUNTAIN GOURD FARM
Route 1, Box 853
Gilmer, TX 75644
(903) 734-5204
http://www.texaseast.com/westmountain
Craft-ready gourds, crafting tools, books

Internet Resources

DO-IT-YOURSELF
http://www.doityourself.com/electric
How-to information and project ideas, Q & A Forum, links to other sites, plus information on other types of do-it-yourself home improvement projects

HOME LIGHTING & ACCESSORIES MAGAZINE
http://www.homelighting.com
Searchable database of lighting manufacturers, suppliers and other sources, plus articles and project ideas

LAMP LINK
http://www.lamplink.com
This site is designed specifically for lamp makers, and offers lamp kits, project ideas, advice, and links to other resources.

Canadian Sources

BIRDS OF PARADISE LAMP SHADES
Marilyn Hodgkinson
112 Sherbourne Street
Toronto, Ontario
M5A 2R2
Custom-made lamp shades. Marilyn does not carry supplies for order, but will craft a shade to meet your specifications.

CANADIAN CRAFT & HOBBY ASSOCIATION
#24 1410 40th Ave., NE
Calgary, Alberta
T2E 6L1
http://www.cdncraft.org
Contact the association or visit their website for information about suppliers in Canada.

RENNICK CRAFT SUPPLIES
#6869 Highway 101
Wirral, New Brunswick
Canada E06 3M0
(506) 687-4734
http://www.angelfire.com/biz/cancraft.html
Lamp shade materials and general craft supplies. Visit their website for links to other Canadian craft suppliers and resources.

Index